Medieval Europe for Kids

A Captivating Guide to the Middle Ages in European History

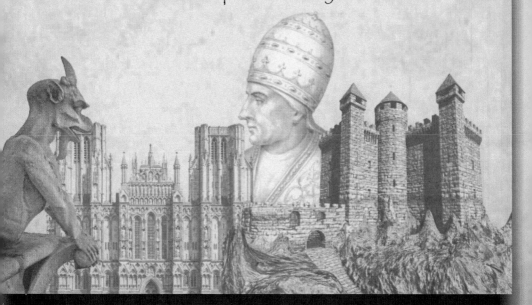

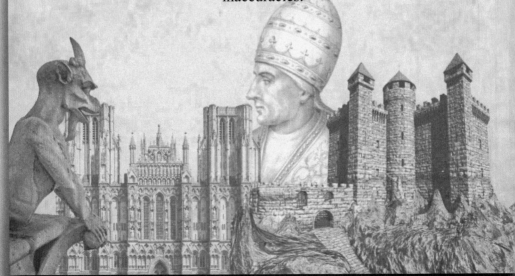

Table of Contents

INTRODUCTION

In this book, we'll explore how people lived in medieval Europe and the incredible legacies they left behind. Discover how the Middle Ages came about and the important people, events, and achievements of this era.

History will come alive with fascinating pictures, fun facts, and interesting activities to make learning exciting and engaging! You'll learn new facts, discover more about things you may have already heard of, and add new words to your vocabulary. There are even helpful pronunciation guides for those tricky new words.

Become an expert on the Middle Ages in no time, and discover a world where fiction and reality are often intertwined!

Chapter 1: How Did the Middle Ages Happen?

The Middle Ages, also known as the *medieval* era, took place in Europe over a period of one thousand years between 500 to 1500 CE. The Middle Ages began shortly after the fall of the Western Roman Empire in 476 CE.

Fun Fact: Historians split the Middle Ages into three different periods. They are the Early Middle Ages (500–1000 CE), the High Middle Ages (1000–1300 CE), and the Late Middle Ages (1300–1500 CE).

The Middle Ages are often referred to as the *Dark Ages* because historians know less about this period than the Romans who came before due to the lack of government records. Much Roman knowledge was lost following the fall of the Roman Empire. It is also called the Dark Ages since many historians in the past suggested the medieval period saw little cultural or scientific advancements. However, you will soon discover this wasn't the case.

Fun Fact: The Romans loved to build roads. They built around 250,000 miles of roads!

Before the Middle Ages, most of Europe was united under Roman control. By 117 CE, the Roman Empire controlled most of Europe and parts of Asia and Africa.

Fun Fact: At its peak, the Roman Empire spanned almost two million square miles. It was home to approximately sixty million people!

A map of the Roman Empire in 117 CE.

When Europe was united under Roman rule, the people experienced relative peace. After the Roman Empire collapsed, Europe entered a period of economic instability. Many countries fought for land and power. Europe was split among different rulers and kingdoms that would often try to conquer one another.

Fun Fact: Although the Western Roman Empire had fallen, the Catholic Church was still very powerful.

In 481, *King Clovis* of France formed the new *Frankish Kingdom,* uniting the tribes in the former Roman *Gaul (gawl)* area. In 711, Islam began to gain popularity in Spain and Portugal. However, Frankish control of the region was cemented with the *Battle of Tours* in 732. In 800, the Frankish *King Charlemagne (shaa-luh-mayn)* was crowned the *Holy Roman emperor.* He united a large part of western Europe, including Germany and France.

In 835, the Vikings, who came from Norway, Denmark, and Sweden, began invading northern Europe. They would continue to do so for over two hundred years. However, they were largely unsuccessful at conquering England. King Alfred the Great defeated the Vikings in 878. England was eventually conquered in 1066 by *William of Normandy* during the *Battle of Hastings*.

The fighting that happened during the Early Middle Ages didn't let up once Europe entered the High Middle Ages. In fact, it got worse! In 1096, the *First Crusade* began. *The Crusades* were a series of holy wars between Christians and Muslims. The wars took place because the Catholic Church wanted to recover the Holy Land of Jerusalem and its surrounding areas, which were under Muslim rule. The land was also sacred to the Muslims, so they did not want to give it up without a fight! There was a total of ten Crusades, which were fought from 1096 to 1291.

A drawing of a medieval knight.

The Crusades are perhaps most remembered because of the knights who fought in them. The famously devout and brutal *Knights Templar* was formed during the Crusades. The Knights Templar proudly displayed a red cross on their banners and armor.

Not long after the Crusades had ended, another war began. The *Hundred Years' War* took place between France and England. It lasted from 1337 to 1453 (more than one hundred years, despite the name!). The war began because the king of England believed he was the rightful heir to the French throne.

One of the most famous figures of the Hundred Years' War was a teenage peasant girl named *Joan of Arc*. When she was twelve years old, Joan had a vision of an angel who told her she would lead the French to victory. She went on to do just that. She successfully led an army at only sixteen! Sadly, Joan of Arc was captured and burned at the stake in 1431 when she was just nineteen years old.

During the Hundred Years' War, a deadly event took place: the *Black Death*. The Black Death was a *bubonic (bew-bon-ik)* plague pandemic that ravaged Europe between 1347 to 1351. The plague was so deadly that it killed about a third of the population of Europe!

Toward the end of the Middle Ages, Europe entered a new period of discovery and learning. Reading and writing became more widely available to everyone thanks to the invention of the printing press around 1436 by *Johannes Gutenberg (yow-ha-nuhs goo-tuhn-buhg)*. The economy improved, and Europe entered the *Renaissance (ruh-nay-sons)*. Great works of art were created. People made inventions and discoveries in the fields of math, science, and medicine. The start of the Renaissance marks the end of the Middle Ages.

Chapter 1 Challenge Activity

Can you place the significant event in the correct place on the timeline?

The Frankish Kingdom is formed

The High Middle Ages

The printing press is invented by Johannes Gutenberg

The Late Middle Ages

The fall of the Western Roman Empire

The Crusades

William of Normandy takes over England in the Battle of Hastings

Joan of Arc is killed

The Black Death

The Hundred Years' War

The Early Middle Ages

The Vikings begin invading Europe

476 -

481 –

500–1000 -

835 -

1000–1300 -

1066 -

1096–1291 -

1300–1500 -

1337–1453 -

1347–1351 -

1431 -

1444 -

476 - The fall of the Western Roman Empire

481 - The Frankish Kingdom is formed

500–1000 - The Early Middle Ages

835 - The Vikings begin invading Europe

1000–1300 - The High Middle Ages

1066 - William of Normandy takes over England in the Battle of Hastings

1096–1291 - The Crusades

1300–1500 - The Late Middle Ages

1337–1453 - The Hundred Years' War

1347–1351 - The Black Death

1431 - Joan of Arc is killed

1436 - The printing press is invented by Johannes Gutenberg

Chapter 2: What Is a Feudal System?

Simply put, a *feudal (fyoo-dl) system* is a type of political system where landowners provide people with some of their lands in exchange for services and loyalty. This is also known as *feudalism (fyoo-dl-ism)*. Feudalism was the main social system in Europe during the Middle Ages.

The feudal system worked in a triangle formation. At the very top was the *monarch* (a king or queen), who was only outranked by God, the pope, and the Catholic Church. The monarch owned most of the land. Since it was too difficult to control alone, the ruling king or queen distributed lands to the barons and nobles in his kingdom.

Fun Fact: The monarch was said to have a "divine right" to the throne, which meant they were appointed by God.

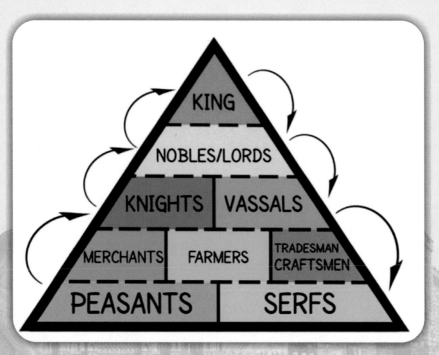

A feudal system pyramid

In the Middle Ages, lands were known as *fiefs (feefs)*. In return for the land, the nobles provided their ruler with knights and soldiers. If they did not have enough soldiers, they paid a tax known as *shield money* instead. The nobles also had to pledge their loyalty to the throne and the monarch's heirs, who would inherit the throne after the ruler died.

Fun Fact: The church also had lands known as dioceses. The highest-ranking church leaders were called bishops. They were responsible for the dioceses.

The nobles divided their fiefs among the lords. The lords were responsible for running the local manors or castles. The crops, peasants, and buildings on these lands belonged to them. The lords' complete control over their fiefs meant they were responsible for coming up with laws and deciding on the punishment if those laws were broken.

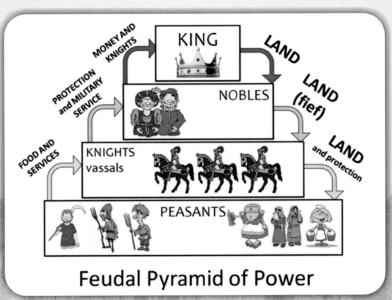

Feudal Pyramid of Power

A drawing of the feudal pyramid of power.

The lords often gave some of their fiefs to a knight or were even knights themselves. The knights provided their lords with loyalty and services in exchange for a small portion of land. The lords provided their knights to the nobles and the king.

Fun Fact: People who were given land by nobles or lords are known as vassals (va-salz).

At the bottom of the pyramid were the peasants and *serfs (surfs)*. They worked the land and offered services and rent in exchange for protection and the ability to live on the fief.

Feudalism was introduced in England by William the Conqueror. After the Battle of Hastings in 1066, William of Normandy was crowned the king of England. He decided to distribute his lands between the church and barons. William kept 20 percent for himself. Twenty-five percent went to the church, and the remaining 55 percent went to the barons who helped him win the war.

The church lands were controlled by the bishops. The bishops and barons had to provide King William with knights when he needed them. They split their lands among undertenants, who paid rent or provided services. The undertenants further split the lands, giving them to peasants or serfs.

If a baron had a lot of land, he had to provide more knights to the king. Whenever William gave a baron a fief, a ceremony took place. The baron would kneel before the king and swear an oath of loyalty for life. The barons demanded similar oaths from their vassals.

Can you draw your own feudal system pyramid? Fill in the triangle below using drawings, names, and descriptions.

Bonus points for using the new words you learned during this chapter: fief, vassal, and serf

Chapter 3: The Great Medieval Castles

When we think of medieval times, we often think of kings, queens, lords, ladies, and knights in castles. This is because many of the castles that are still standing in Europe were built during the Middle Ages. There were three main types of castles. In the beginning, there were *motte-and-bailey* castles. Later, there were *stone keep castles* and *concentric castles*.

The different types of castles

Motte and Bailey

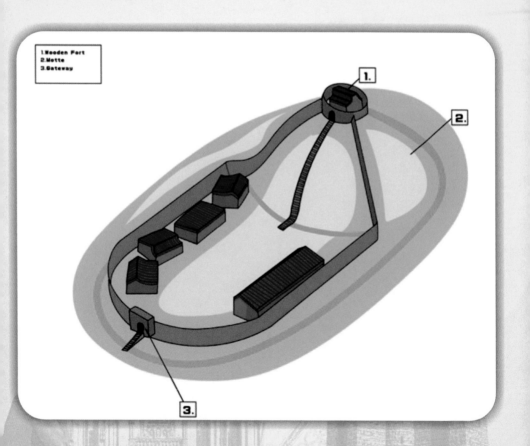

1.Wooden Fort
2.Motte
3.Gateway

Stone Keep

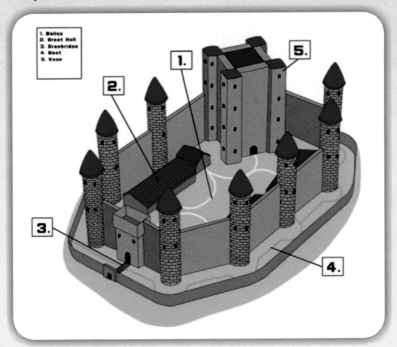

1. Bailey
2. Great Hall
3. Drawbridge
4. Moat
5. Keep

Concentric

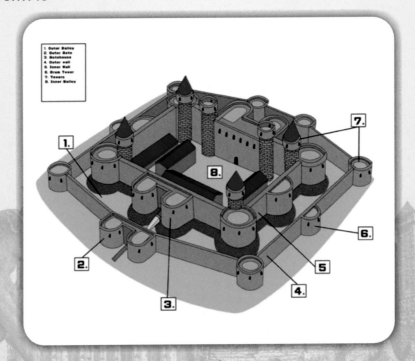

1. Outer Bailey
2. Outer Gate
3. Gatehouse
4. Outer wall
5. Inner Hall
6. Drum Tower
7. Towers
8. Inner Bailey

Motte-and-bailey castles were one of the first kinds of castles in England. They were originally made from wood. As you may have guessed, these castles were made up of two different parts: the motte *(maht)* and the bailey.

The motte was a raised pile of earth or a hill with a wooden or stone keep on top of it. The keep was a tower. People would take refuge there if the castle was under attack. Keeps had steep sides to make them very difficult to climb. The mottes could be anywhere between twenty-five to eighty feet high and had a flat top. Mottes could either be naturally formed or manmade.

Fun Fact: Wooden keeps were more vulnerable to attack since they could be set on fire. A keep would be covered in animal hides to protect it from fire.

An illustration of a motte-and-bailey castle.
https://commons.wikimedia.org/wiki/File:Motte_Strichzeichnung.png

Motte-and-bailey castles were very quick and easy to build. The Normans loved this style so much that four out of five castles were built in this style!

The bailey was a courtyard surrounded by walls, a *palisade* (a fence made out of wooden stakes), and a deep ditch known as a *fosse (fos)*. The ditch could be filled with water to make a *moat*. The baileys were quite large. The peasants and workers of the castle would live in the bailey. There would also be shops, stables, storerooms, and soldiers' quarters.

Some of the most famous castles in England were built by William the Conqueror. Perhaps his most famous castles are Windsor Castle and the Tower of London. Windsor Castle is an example of a motte-and-bailey castle. It is still used as one of the English monarch's residences. It was originally made from wood. It was later modernized and built from stone.

The motte at Warwick Castle
https://pixabay.com/photos/warwick-castle-fort-warwick-castle-2484196/

The motte-and-bailey castle lost its popularity. By 1200, no new ones were being built. It was more vulnerable to attacks than the stone castles that followed. Wooden keeps were vulnerable to fire and attacks, and they also weren't ideal for the British weather. Over time, the rain caused the wood to rot, which made the building structurally unsound. They weren't particularly cozy places to live since you couldn't light a fire in the winter!

Stone castles solved these issues. They were strong, long-lasting, weatherproof, fireproof, and more impressive. While they may have been more expensive and harder to build than their wooden counterparts, this wasn't necessarily seen as a bad thing. The nobles saw stone castles as a sign of their wealth and power. If a keep was impressive and safe, the people were more likely to be obedient.

The lord and lady of the castle usually lived in the keep on the level called the *solar*. There was also a great hall for entertaining guests and housing people should the castle come under attack. On the lower levels were the kitchens and a cellar. There was also a chapel within the castle walls.

Fun Fact: Stone keeps were initially rectangular. Later, they became circular.

There were *battlements* along the top and arrow slits for archers to shoot at enemies. A *forebuilding* protected the entrance of the keep. There was also a gatehouse with guards to protect the entrance should anyone get past the moat. A drawbridge could be pulled up and down to allow people in and keep enemies out.

The keep was surrounded by a thick wall made of stone called the *curtain wall*. There were *turrets* along the curtain wall. Turrets were towers used as lookouts for any oncoming attacks. Within the curtain wall was a bailey with stables.

The concentric castle went one step further than the stone keep castles. These castles were practically the same as stone keeps but had two walls protecting the castle instead of just one. These two walls are known as the outer wall and inner wall. Perhaps the most famous example of a concentric castle is the Tower of London. It was originally a stone keep. The outer wall was later added for extra protection, making it a concentric castle.

A photo of the Tower of London today. You can see the White Tower (the keep) in the middle and both curtain walls.

Chapter 3 Activity

Draw your own medieval castle and label the main areas. Be sure to include some of the new terms you learned in this chapter, such as moat, motte, bailey, keep, curtain walls, turrets, battlements, drawbridge, forebuilding, or fosse.

Chapter 4: A Knight's Tale

Chances are you've probably already heard of knights. They're one of the most famous parts of medieval history. You have probably seen them on TV or in movies. Maybe you read about them in books. Many of these stories feature brave knights fighting dragons and saving princesses. But did you know that knights were actually real? Okay, so maybe they weren't running around slaying dragons. But they were a type of soldier during the medieval period.

There were three different types of soldiers in the Middle Ages. The knights were at the top. Below them were archers and foot soldiers. Knights wore heavy armor and rode on horses into battle. Only very rich nobles could afford to become a knight since weapons, armor, and horses were expensive to buy.

Fun Fact: Knights first became popular under King Charlemagne of the Franks in the 700s. Charlemagne rewarded his best knights with land. In return for the land, the knights pledged to fight for King Charlemagne whenever he needed them. This practice was later adopted and became the feudal system.

Knights were expected to follow certain rules and behave according to the *Code of Chivalry (shi-vuhl-ree)*. Knights were expected to be good Christians. They had to be brave, loyal, and polite. They protected the church, their king, women, and the weak. Knights were expected to be fair and honest. Many knights followed the code, but not all of them were good at maintaining it.

There were two ways to become a knight. If a soldier fought bravely, he could be awarded the title by the king, a lord, or another knight. The other way was to become an apprentice to a knight. Through hard work and training, they might eventually be considered worthy of the title. Because of the high cost of being a knight, apprentices mostly came from aristocratic or noble families.

Fun Fact: People can still be awarded a knighthood today. However, they get these for political and social achievements and charitable contributions, not for fighting. Some celebrities who have been awarded a knighthood include singer Elton John, inventor Bill Gates, US President Ronald Reagan, and actor Angelina Jolie.

A drawing of a medieval knight.
https://commons.wikimedia.org/w/index.php?curid=865123

Being a knight's apprentice was not an easy task. Apprentices had to move away from home to start training at only seven years old. They became *pages*. Pages were essentially servants. They had to help the knight with household tasks, such as washing clothes, serving meals, and delivering messages. They would also be taught how to behave properly, how to ride a horse while carrying a *lance* (a long weapon), and how to fight using wooden swords and shields.

Once a page turned fifteen, he would become a *squire*. Squires were given the added responsibility of caring for the knight's most prized possessions: his weapons, armor, and horses. Squires were expected to know how to fight with real weapons. They also needed to practice fighting on horseback. Squires would also get their first taste of a real battlefield by going there with the knight.

Fun Fact: The richest knights had lots of pages and squires serving them.

After about five or six years of training, a squire could be given the title of a knight in a *dubbing ceremony*. During the ceremony, a knight, lord, or even the king would knight those shown to be brave enough. A sword would be tapped on both shoulders as the new knight swore an *oath of fealty* (a promise to be loyal) to the king and church. As a token of his new title, the new knight would be given a pair of riding spurs and a sword.

When there were no wars or battles, knights had to find another way to practice their skills. This led to the introduction of *tournaments* and *jousting (jowst-ing)*. The town hosting the tournament would invite knights from other areas to come and compete in pretend battles. Large groups of spectators would come to watch and cheer their favorites.

The main event of the tournament was the *joust*. Two knights on horseback would charge toward each other while holding wooden lances. Their goal was to knock their opponent off their horse. The winner would be awarded prize money. Sometimes, the winner even won their opponent's horse and armor!

Tournaments were a great way for a knight to become rich. Knights who became very wealthy or who were older often chose to pay a *shield tax* to the king to buy soldiers instead of fighting themselves.

Fun Fact: Jousts were very dangerous and could result in injury or even death. The wooden lances had blunted ends, but that didn't make it safe. King Henry II died during a joust in 1559!

A drawing of a joust.

When knights were in their armor, it was very hard for the spectators to tell them apart. So, the knights began painting symbols on their shields so people could tell who was who. The knights would later paint these onto banners and the cloaks they wore over their armor. This was called a *coat of arms*. A coat of arms was a symbol that represented a family. Both knights and nobles had them.

There were so many knights that it became hard to keep track of who had which symbol. So, a new job, a *herald (heh-ruhld)*, was made to keep track of them. Heralds ensured that no two families had the same coat of arms and kept track of which symbol belonged to whom.

In the beginning, coats of arms were fairly simple. Over time, they became more elaborate to ensure they were different. A coat of arms included several things. There was an *escutcheon (uh-skuht-shn)*, which was the shape of the arms. A *field* was the background colors or patterns. Inside this were designs known as *ordinaries*. Finally, there was also a *charge*. This was a special symbol. It was often an animal or object. The color or charge on the coat of arms had different meanings.

The Royal Arms of England, King Richard I coat of arms.

Chapter 4 Activity

Can you fill in the blanks?

Knights were a type of _____ who lived in medieval times and fought on horseback. To become a knight, you had to be very rich. Their _____, weapons, and horses were very expensive. Knights could earn the title by being _____ in battle or by doing an apprenticeship with a knight. Apprentices started serving their knights as a _____ when they were seven. When they were fifteen, they would graduate to become a _____ and start using real weapons. When they were around twenty-one, they would become a knight in a _____ ceremony. They would swear an oath of _____ to the king and church.

Knights lived by a Code of _____, which meant they had to behave in an honorable way. They had to be honest, brave, and polite. They had to protect the church, the king, women, and the weak. When they weren't fighting battles, they fought in _____. The main event was the _____. Two knights would charge at each other while riding on horseback and carrying _____. They had to knock the other rider off their _____. Knights wore their _____ of _____ to show who they were. This would be passed down from generation to generation. There were _____ to keep track of whose symbol belonged to whom.

Chapter 4 Answer

Can you fill in the blanks?

Knights were a type of <u>soldier</u> who lived in medieval times and fought on horseback. To become a knight, you had to be very rich. Their <u>armor</u>, weapons, and horses were very expensive. Knights could earn the title by being <u>brave</u> in battle or by doing an apprenticeship with a knight. Apprentices started serving their knights as a <u>page</u> when they were seven. When they were fifteen, they would graduate to become a squire and start using real weapons. When they were around twenty-one, they would become a knight in a <u>dubbing</u> ceremony. They would swear an oath of <u>fealty (or loyalty)</u> to the king and church.

Knights lived by a Code of <u>Chivalry</u>, which meant where they had to behave in an honorable way. They had to be honest, brave, and polite. They had to protect the church, the king, women, and the weak. When they weren't fighting battles, they fought in <u>tournaments</u>. The main event was the <u>joust</u>. Two knights would charge at each other while riding on horseback and carrying <u>lances</u>. They had to knock the other rider off their <u>horse</u>. Knights wore their coat of <u>arms</u> to show who they were. This would be passed down from generation to generation. There were <u>heralds</u> to keep track of whose symbol belonged to whom.

Chapter 5: Town Life: Trade, Guilds, and Craftsmen

During the Middle Ages, most people lived in the countryside and worked as farmers as part of the manor or castle. However, there were also larger towns and cities. The towns were very crowded and dirty. They did not have proper *sanitation* (ways to clean themselves well). People threw their toilet waste and trash into the streets and rivers. Animals also roamed the streets. All of this meant diseases spread quite easily.

Medieval cities and towns would usually be by a river. The river provided people with water for drinking and bathing. The people also dumped their sewage in the river. In the Middle Ages, populations were small by today's standards. In 1300, London had a population of only eighty thousand people. In 2019, London had a population of over eight million!

However, medieval cities and towns were still very crowded since they were often built on a small area of land. The roads were very narrow. Small houses were clustered together with no space between them. Second stories jutted out to make more space. Lots of houses were made from wood, which meant fires could easily spread.

Fun Fact: The Great Fire of London in 1666 decimated the city and destroyed several landmarks. St Paul's Cathedral, eighty-seven churches, and over thirteen thousand homes burned down.

Medieval cities and towns were circular and had stone walls with turrets for protection. Within the walls, there would be at least one church, a town square, and *guild halls*. In guild halls, *guilds (gildz)* met. Guild halls were often used as shelter if the city was under attack. Churches and guild halls were usually located near the city walls.

A Map of Medieval Paris, France.
https://pixabay.com/vectors/map-paris-medieval-line-art-5616856/

In the towns and cities, men worked as craftsmen, merchants, doctors, lawyers, or servants. Women usually stayed at home to raise the children and perform household tasks. A few worked as shopkeepers, seamstresses, or maids. Some even ran taverns. Craftsmen were skilled workers. There were blacksmiths, carpenters, *cobblers* (shoemakers), bakers, bookbinders, candlestick makers, weavers, and more. In the Middle Ages, a craftsman would be a member of a guild. Guilds were groups containing other people in the same trade.

There were many different types of crafts. In a big city, there could be a hundred different guilds!

Guilds were important. They enabled craftsmen to pass on their skills and knowledge. The members also supported each other, which was especially helpful in times of need. The guilds controlled the number of hours a craftsman could work and the working conditions. They also prevented non-members from selling goods. Certain members didn't even have to pay taxes. Customers also benefited from guilds since guilds made sure members were selling good products for a reasonable price.

People had to pay a fee to be a member of a guild.

Guilds ran apprenticeships. Teenage apprentices would sign up to train with a *master* for seven years. They worked for a master in exchange for learning the craft. They would be given food, *board* (a room to stay), and clothing. Once an apprentice completed his training, he became a *journeyman*. As a journeyman, he continued to work for his master but would be paid.

A painting of a medieval baker and his apprentice.
https://commons.wikimedia.org/w/index.php?curid=1197015

A journeyman could not become a master without the guild's approval. To get this, a journeyman would have to prove his skill and abide by the guild's rules. They also had to produce a masterpiece for the guild to review and approve. If a journeyman became a master, he would be allowed his own shop and apprentices.

There were also merchant guilds for *tradesmen* (merchants). Merchant guilds could become rich and powerful. Trade was an important and money-making business. Merchants would get supplies from neighboring cities and countries.

Only the most powerful guilds had guild halls. Guild halls were used to hold meetings and punish people who broke the rules.

Fun Fact: Even though women could learn a skilled craft, they were forbidden from joining or creating a guild.

Medieval guilds, trade, and even towns could not be created without the monarch's permission. The monarch had to issue a royal *charter*. A charter was a special document that allowed certain things to happen. Towns and cities needed charters to choose their government and pass judgment on criminals. They also needed permission to have markets or form guilds.

The most famous medieval charter is the *Magna Carta*. The Magna Carta is one of the most important charters in the history of democracy. King John of England was forced to sign it in 1215. It declared the king was not above the law and had a duty to protect his people. The Magna Carta included things like forming a council to ensure the king followed the law. It protected the rights of the church and put limits on taxes and feudal payments.

A painting of King John signing the Magna Carta.
https://commons.wikimedia.org/w/index.php?curid=91755225

Can you fill in the crossword using the clues below?

1. After finishing your apprenticeship to become a master craftsman, you would become a...

2. Craftsmen formed groups known as this.

3. King John of England had to sign this document. It is considered one of the most important documents in the history of democracy.

4. Medieval streets were very...

5. A special document issued by the king to grant permission to do something, such as having a market or government.

6. All medieval towns had at least one of these religious buildings.

Chapter 5 Answer

	1.	J								
		O						5.	C	
2.	G	U	I	L	D				H	
		R							A	
		N		6.	C	H	U	R	C	H
		E							T	
		Y							E	
	3.	M	A	G	N	A	C	A	R	T	A
		A								
	4.	N	A	R	R	O	W			

33

Chapter 6: Peasants and Serfs

We've already briefly mentioned peasants and serfs. They were at the bottom of the feudal pyramid. In this chapter, we're going to discover what life would be like if you were part of the lower classes in medieval Europe.

Fun Fact: All serfs were peasants, but not all peasants were serfs.

Peasants and serfs were poor. They commonly lived on the lands of manors or castles. They worked, planted crops, or tended to the livestock.

A painting of peasants working in the fields.
https://commons.wikimedia.org/w/index.php?curid=16340916

Peasants owned land or businesses, but serfs did not. Peasants were above serfs in the social *hierarchy* (a system that ranks people by their status in society). Peasants were still very poor. They had to work two or three days a week on their lord's land. Peasants also had to pay taxes. If they used the land for themselves, they would be arrested. They could even be sentenced to death for killing a deer!

The serfs were the lowest social class. They did not own anything. Serfs needed permission from their lord to leave the land. They also had to buy their freedom. If the land a serf lived on was sold, the new owner would own them. Serfs had to work at least six days a week. They barely had enough food to survive since most of the crops they grew belonged to their lord. It was a hard life. Many serfs didn't live past thirty.

Fun Fact: Around 85 percent of the population were peasants or serfs.

Serfs and peasants didn't just work as farmers. Some of the more skilled peasants owned businesses. Peasants could be butchers, bakers, blacksmiths, or carpenters. Serfs could not own a business, but they worked in these jobs and belonged to the business.

Serfs may have been below peasants in the social hierarchy, but their lives weren't too different. Most peasants lived in small one- or two-room houses. The whole family lived there, so it was very crowded. Everyone slept in the same room. Even the farm animals lived inside! The houses would be dark and filled with smoke from the fire.

Houses were made using *wattle and daub*. Vertical wooden stakes (*wattles*) were woven with branches and twigs to make a wall. This was then stuck together (*daubed*) with mud, clay, animal dung, and straw.

Fun Fact: The wattle and daub method has been used for over six thousand years. It is still used in some parts of the world today.

An old wattle and daub church in Romania.

Sumptuary (suhmp-choo-uh-ree) laws *forbade* (banned) peasants from wearing the same clothes as nobles. Certain styles and materials were only for the rich. Peasants wore wool clothing to keep them warm in the winter.

A peasant's diet was very basic. They could not afford meat, eggs, or cheese on a daily basis. They had to eat fresh food since they didn't have refrigerators. They often ate bread and vegetable stew. The bread was not soft like the bread we eat today. It was coarse and gritty. It ground people's teeth down. Most people only drank ale (a type of beer) since the water made them sick.

A painting of peasants eating.
https://commons.wikimedia.org/w/index.php?curid=1859446

Can you tell which sentences describe a peasant and which a serf?

Peasant   **Serf**

Bound to the land and cannot leave without permission from their lord.

Not bound to the land and free to move.

Owned land.

Did not own land.

The lowest in the social hierarchy.

The second-lowest in the social hierarchy.

Is only a peasant.

Is also a peasant.

Chapter 6 Answer

Peasant	Serf
Not bound to the land and free to move.	Bound to the land and cannot leave without permission from their lord.
Owned land.	Did not own land.
The second-lowest in the social hierarchy.	The lowest in the social hierarchy.
Is only a peasant.	Is also a peasant.

Chapter 7: The Medieval Church

Religion was incredibly important in medieval Europe. Europe was even nicknamed *Christendom*, which meant "kingdom of Christ." The biggest religion in Europe was Christianity. The Catholic Church was very powerful.

Fun Fact: Not everyone in Europe was Christian. Spain was occupied by Muslims. Vikings believed in the Old Norse gods like Thor. There were also many Jews living throughout Europe.

The church was involved in every aspect of life during the Middle Ages. It even *confirmed* (gave the religious right to rule) kings. This meant the king was a *divine ruler* appointed by God. The church owned around one-third of all of the lands in western Europe. The church was independent of the king, so it did not have to pay taxes like everyone else. People had to pay the church one-tenth of their annual income. This was called a *tithe (ti-the)*.

People also had to pay the church for various ceremonies. They had to pay for weddings, communions, baptisms, funerals, and burials. If someone had done something wrong, they had to show their *remorse* (how sorry they were) by paying *penances (peh-nuhn-suhz)* to the church. A person confessed their sins to a priest in return for forgiveness from God. Penances were often paid. Rich nobles also gave the church lands as gifts or penance. The church was very wealthy and powerful.

The leader of the Catholic Church was the pope. The pope was considered to be God's highest representative on earth. The pope decided what things were spiritually important. He had to choose the official *doctrine* (beliefs) that would be taught. The pope wore beautiful robes with gold and jewels on them.

The Roman Catholic Church was based in Rome. In medieval times, the pope lived in the *Lateran Palace*. In the 14th century, he moved to the *Vatican*. Today, the pope lives in the Vatican. He is still the leader of the Catholic Church.

INNOCENTIVS ·VII·PP·SVLMO·

A drawing of one of the most famous medieval Popes, Pope Innocent VII.
https://commons.wikimedia.org/w/index.php?curid=52373259

Below the pope were *cardinals (kar-duh-nuhlz)*. Then there were bishops and abbots. There were also priests, monks, and nuns. Bishops were the heads of local parishes and had a lot of power. They would often be on the king's council. Priests assisted bishops. Priests were responsible for running churches on the manors. They would *absolve* (forgive) people of their sins during confession and oversee religious ceremonies. They also passed on messages from the pope or bishop.

Abbots were the heads of *monasteries (mo-nuh-stare-eez)*. Below them was a *prior*. Monks lived in monasteries. Monks devoted their lives to prayer. The monastery provided everything the monks needed, so they never had to leave. They grew their own crops and made their own clothes. They were *isolated* (lived on their own) from the outside world.

Monasteries contained several buildings. There were sleeping quarters, bathrooms, kitchens, and a chapel. There was a large hall called the *refectory (ruh-fek-tuh-ree)*, where the monks ate, and a *warming room* with a fire. The *chapter house* was where the heads of the monastery met to discuss issues. There was also a library and various other rooms, such as a room where the choir practiced. In the middle of the monastery was a garden. Around the garden's edge was a covered walkway called a *cloister (kloy-stur)*. The monks used the cloister to move around and get exercise. They also used it as a place to study.

Fun Fact: An abbey is a type of monastery.

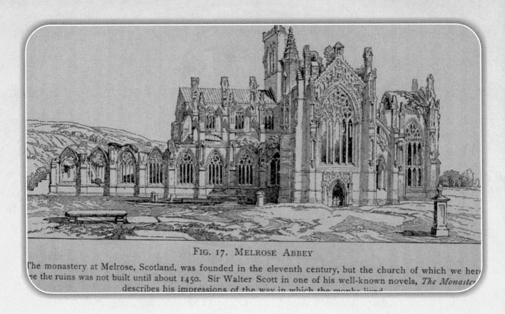

FIG. 17. MELROSE ABBEY

The monastery at Melrose, Scotland, was founded in the eleventh century, but the church of which we her[e] [s]ee the ruins was not built until about 1450. Sir Walter Scott in one of his well-known novels, *The Monaste*[ry] describes his impressions of the way in which the monks lived

A picture of Melrose Abbey, Scotland.
Internet Archive Book Images, No restrictions, via Wikimedia Commons,
https://commons.wikimedia.org/w/index.php?curid=41878641

Monks were some of the only people who could read and write. It was their job to share their knowledge of God with the world. They wrote lots of books and kept records of important events. Without monks, historians wouldn't know much about the Middle Ages.

Although monks were isolated, they still had some interaction with the outside world. Monks taught boys in the community. They also cared for the sick and fed the poor. In the Middle Ages, hotels didn't exist, so weary travelers stayed at monasteries.

A monk's day was full of praying, studying the Bible, and doing chores. Their chores depended on what they were good at or enjoyed. Some monks were in charge of the food. Others were in charge of making, mending, or washing clothing. Some worked as *scribes*. They wrote records or copied important documents. It could take a whole year for a scribe to copy the Bible. The monk in charge of all the books was a *sacrist*. There was also the *cantor* who led the choir and the *lector* who led the lessons.

To become a monk, you had to dedicate yourself to God. Monks vowed to devote their lives to the monastery. They gave up their worldly goods (*possessions*). Monks promised to be *obedient* (do as they are told) and live a life of *chastity* (not to marry or have relationships with women). Because monks did not have belongings and led simple lives, they all wore the same clothes. Monks wore brown woolen robes with hoods and a rope tied around their waists. They often shaved a bald patch on the top of their heads to show *humility* (that they were *modest* or not proud).

Fun Fact: Monks didn't speak much. In fact, some even took a vow of silence!

A picture of a medieval monk.
https://commons.wikimedia.org/w/index.php?curid=18478996

There were also *friars (fry-ers)*. A friar took many of the same vows as monks. But they lived in society among regular people. Friars taught the children of the community about religion and music. They also helped care for the poor, sick, and elderly. They recorded their missions and reported back to the church.

Friars were well respected within the community. They led modest lives and gave up worldly goods. Friars wore similar clothing to monks and carried rosary beads. Friars could not have money and had to rely on the charity of others. They could only eat or wear things that were given to them.

Nuns were similar to monks. The main difference was that they were women. Nuns lived in *convents*. Nuns were not as educated as monks, but some could read and write. Widows, young women without a husband, or women who were seen as being immoral were sent to convents. Others chose to devote their lives to God.

Nuns wore long robes in black, grey, or white. They tied their robes with a cloth or leather belt. They wore a *scapular (ska-pyuh-lr)* over their dress. A scapular was a long white piece of cloth that hung down at the front and back. Many nuns wore *rosary beads*, which were a type of beaded necklace with a cross at the end. The beads were used to count their penances. Nuns covered their heads with a piece of cloth called a *wimple*.

Fun Fact: It was very common for nuns to shave their heads!

A painting of two medieval nuns.
https://commons.wikimedia.org/w/index.php?curid=71677402

Chapter 7 Activity

Time to test how many new words you've learned. Try to remember the correct word for the descriptions below.

1. The place where monks lived.

2. Similar to a monk but lived in society.

3. The covered walkway around the garden where monks lived.

4. You paid these to show how sorry you were.

5. People paid these to the church. It made up one-tenth of their income.

6. Europe's nickname that meant "divine kingdom."

7. A special type of necklace with beads and a cross at the end.

8. The places where nuns lived.

1. The place where monks lived. A monastery or monasteries (plural)

2. Similar to a monk but lived in society. Friars

3. The covered walkway around the garden where monks lived. The cloister

4. You paid these to show how sorry you were. Penances

5. People paid these to the church. It made up one-tenth of their income. Tithes

6. Europe's nickname that meant "divine kingdom." Christendom

7. A special type of necklace with beads and a cross at the end. Rosary beads

8. The places where nuns lived. Convents

It's important to remember the Middle Ages lasted over one thousand years! Europe is a large continent with many different countries and cultures. This means medieval art and architecture are quite varied. The style of art depended on the time and location. Generally, medieval art is divided into three different styles and periods: *Byzantine (bi-zuhn-teen) art, Romanesque (row-muh-nesk) art,* and *Gothic (gaa-thuhk) art.*

Many works of art were religious because of the church's importance. Paintings, engravings, sculptures, metalwork, and stained glass are all examples of the types of art made in the Middle Ages.

The first kind of style was Byzantine art. This type of art was popular from roughly 500 to 1000 CE. It is called Byzantine art since the artists mostly came from the Eastern Roman Empire, which is also called the *Byzantine Empire.* Byzantine art featured many religious images, especially of Jesus and the Virgin Mary.

A Byzantine painting of two saints and Christ at the top.
https://commons.wikimedia.org/w/index.php?curid=97440897

Byzantine art wasn't very realistic. The artists wanted the symbolic message to be more important. These paintings are usually two-dimensional without shadows. The people in the paintings look very serious.

Romanesque art was made between 1000 and 1300 CE. Romanesque art was influenced by Byzantine art and Roman art. It heavily focused on religious imagery. Romanesque artists revived the art of *monumental sculptures* (large sculptures). Romanesque art was also featured in architecture. Buildings had stained glass windows, *intricate* (complex) carvings, and large murals. Romanesque architecture was characterized by round arches, small windows, and thick stone walls. Romanesque ceilings were *barrel-vaulted*. This meant they were curved and looked a bit like a tunnel. This technique was first used by the Romans. The walls had to be thick and large to support the ceilings. These buildings had heavy pillars called *piers*.

Romanesque-style doorway.
https://commons.wikimedia.org/w/index.php?curid=82272215

Gothic art developed toward the end of the Romanesque art movement. Gothic art was more realistic. It used more shadow and light. Gothic artists also moved away from only using religious imagery. They began using animals and landscape scenes.

Gothic architecture featured *vaulted ceilings* (high ceilings) with pointed arches. Gothic buildings had thinner pillars than Romanesque buildings. Gothic buildings are also famous for their *spires*. Spires are the tall pointed part at the top of a tower. Spires symbolized the building reaching toward the heavens.

Gothic buildings often had *gargoyles (gar-goylz)*. These were frighting monstrous-looking sculptures that sat near the top of a building. It is likely they were designed to scare demons away. However, they had a practical purpose. Many gargoyles worked as waterspouts that drained rainwater away from the building. Gargoyles were commonly used in churches and cathedrals.

A photo of Notre-Dame.

Some of the most famous gargoyles are outside Notre-Dame (no-truh-daam), a cathedral in Paris. Notre-Dame is one of the oldest Gothic cathedrals in the world.

A photo of a gargoyle at Notre-Dame.
Pedro Lastra peterlaster, CC0, via Wikimedia Commons,
https://commons.wikimedia.org/w/index.php?curid=61900111

Medieval literature was mostly produced by monks and religious people since few people could read and write. This meant the majority of literature was religious. One of the most famous religious-themed poems was written by *Dante Alighieri (dahn-tay a-luh-gee-ree)* in 1320. It is called the *Divine Comedy*. It discussed Dante's ideas of the afterlife. It is considered one of the greatest works of literature.

There were also non-religious works. In 1387, *Geoffrey Chaucer (chaa-sr)* released the first story of *The Canterbury Tales*. The *Canterbury Tales* is a collection of short stories that give us insight into life in England during the Middle Ages. It was one of the first books to be written in English. Chaucer's stories became so popular that he was even invited to court to read them to the king. *The Canterbury Tales* is still studied and read around the world.

Another famous fictional story is the tale of *Beowulf (bay-ow-wolf)*. *Beowulf* is an old English poem set in Scandinavia. It is not known who wrote it. It was likely told for years before being written down sometime at the start of the 11th century. This would make it thousands of years old! The tale follows the hero Beowulf as he fights two monsters and a dragon. It is one of the most important works of Old English literature.

Fun Fact: It is thanks to the Middle Ages that illustrated books with drawings exist. Because many people could not read, it became standard practice to include drawings to clearly show what the text said.

It's time to get creative! You decide what you want to do! You could draw a picture of a Gothic building, complete with spires, gargoyles, and archways. Or how about writing your very own epic medieval short story with heroes, princesses, and dragons? Not sure what to do? Color in the gargoyle below.

Chapter 9: A Plague Most Deadly

One of the most significant events of the Middle Ages took place between 1347 to 1350 in Europe. It is known as the *Black Death*. The Black Death was a *pandemic* (a disease that affects many countries). A disease called the *bubonic (bew-bon-ik) plague* killed at least a third of the population of Europe. It killed anywhere between seventy-five to two hundred million people!

The plague was incredibly *contagious* (easy to catch). There was no cure if you caught it. Medicine wasn't as advanced as it is nowadays. Approximately 60 percent of people who caught it died. People were very scared. They thought the plague was sent as a punishment

Although this outfit didn't become popular until the
17th century, this is what a plague doctor looked like.
Korneevyshka, CC BY-SA 3.0 <https://creativecommons.org/licenses/by-sa/3.0>,
via Wikimedia Commons, https://commons.wikimedia.org/w/index.php?curid=50983452

from God. They also thought the plague was spread through bad smells. Doctors wore strange masks that looked like beaks. At the end of the beak, they put strong-smelling herbs, spices, vinegar, or flowers. However, bad smells were not to blame. The real culprits were infected fleas and lice.

Infected fleas and lice jumped from human to human. Rats and other animals also helped spread the disease. The plague spread quickly. It sometimes wiped out entire populations! People would die within twelve hours to one week after being infected. To stop the spread of the disease, people tried *quarantining* (isolating themselves) and burning the dead. This helped but not before killing millions.

Fun Fact: In Paris, France, an estimated eight hundred people died every day from the plague. There were so many dead bodies that there wasn't enough space to bury everyone.

A medieval painting of the Black Death.
https://commons.wikimedia.org/w/index.php?curid=84268633

The bubonic plague still exists today. It occasionally reappears. Due to advancements in medicine, the bubonic plague is not as deadly as it was in the Middle Ages. Back in medieval times, many ideas for causes and treatments of diseases were based on religion and superstition. The church said people who became sick were being punished by God. Rather than seeking practical solutions to illness or injuries, the people prayed for God's forgiveness and hoped they would be healed.

Fun Fact: People didn't live long in medieval times. The average life expectancy was only thirty to thirty-five years old. Giving birth was very dangerous for both the mother and the baby. One in five children died during childbirth.

People believed the body was made up of the *four humors*. The four humors were yellow and black *bile* (digestive fluids), *phlegm (flem)* (a type of mucus made in your chest), and blood. The four humors were controlled by the four natural elements: earth, water, air, and fire. It was thought that if your humors were unbalanced, you would become sick. A common treatment for many illnesses was to bleed people using sharp objects or *leeches* (a type of bloodsucking worm). They believed you would feel better by getting rid of *excess* (extra) blood. This method was called *bloodletting*.

Astrology (the belief that the position of the planets and things in space influence people on earth) also impacted medieval medicine. Doctors checked the position of the planets to determine when to treat a patient. They also believed the position of the moon could influence the fluids in the body.

People would go to an *apothecary* (a person who made and sold medicine out of herbs and plants) to buy various potions and remedies. If you had a broken bone, needed a tooth pulled, or required minor surgery, then you would go to a barber-surgeon. Barber-surgeons performed surgeries because they already had the sharp tools needed to do it. They also used them for cutting and shaving hair!

Fun Fact: You probably wouldn't want to go to a barber-surgeon for a haircut. They often washed a person's hair with urine if they were short of soap!

A medieval painting of a man having a tooth pulled by a barber-surgeon.
https://commons.wikimedia.org/w/index.php?curid=4552580

Chapter 9 Activity

1. What was the bubonic plague also known as?

2. What animal part did a plague doctor's mask resemble?

3. What was the real cause of the spread of the bubonic plague?

4. What were the four humors?

5. As well as cutting hair, what else did medieval barbers do?

6. What were leeches used for?

Chapter 9 Answer

1. What was the bubonic plague also known as? The Black Death.

2. What animal part did a plague doctor's mask resemble? A beak.

3. What was the real cause of the spread of the bubonic plague? Infected fleas and lice.

4. What were the four humors? Yellow bile, black bile, phlegm, and blood.

5. As well as cutting hair, what else did medieval barbers do? They performed minor surgeries. They were called barber-surgeons.

6. What were leeches used for? Bloodletting. They removed excess blood from a person.

Chapter 10: The Middle Ages: A Lasting Legacy

After the Middle Ages, Europe entered the Renaissance. The Renaissance was a cultural movement that rediscovered the art, literature, science, and philosophies of ancient Greece and Rome. Renaissance scholars were the first people to use the term "Middle Ages." Because of their love of Roman and Greek works, the Renaissance scholars saw the Middle Ages as a period of decline where nothing much happened. They saw people who lived during the Middle Ages as *ignorant* (uneducated) and superstitious.

Today, historians know this is not true. Lots of important changes took place during the Middle Ages. New social and political organizations emerged. Beautiful works of Gothic architecture were built. Important works of art and literature were created. Medieval Europe was also responsible for the world's first universities.

A painting showing a snapshot of medieval life.
https://commons.wikimedia.org/w/index.php?curid=76657640

The legacy of the Roman Catholic Church was also important. Catholicism is still thriving today. At the end of the Middle Ages, the Church of England was established by King Henry VIII. King Henry wanted to *annul* (cancel) his marriage with his wife, Catherine of Aragon. But the Catholic Church wouldn't allow it. Instead of taking no for an answer, Henry established a *Protestant (praa-tuh-stnt)* church. *Protestantism* is the second-most practiced form of Christianity in the world after Catholicism. It is the most popular form of Christianity in the United States.

A painting of a Gothic cathedral in a medieval town.
https://commons.wikimedia.org/w/index.php?curid=7174672

When we think of the Middle Ages today, there are many lasting influences. There are the beautiful churches, cathedrals, abbeys, and castles that are still visited by thousands of people. There are great works of literature and art. Medieval culture has also had a big impact on popular TV shows and movies. Movies and shows feature medieval-inspired characters, such as knights, royalty, magical and superstitious ideas, and mythical monsters like dragons.

While we might have moved on as a society in lots of ways (especially when it comes to medicine, science, and technology), there are still influences in modern culture we can attribute to medieval culture. Ideas of chivalry and protecting women, the sick, and the elderly are still fairly commonplace within Western society. We may not live in a feudal society today. But the ideas of buying and selling land, working for a living, and paying taxes all still exist and are practiced today.

Medieval agricultural calendar from a manuscript
of Pietro Crescenzi, written c. 1306.
https://commons.wikimedia.org/w/index.php?curid=1949466

There were a number of significant inventions and developments during the Middle Ages, especially in farming and agriculture. The Middle Ages saw the inventions of the mechanical clock, the dry compass, and spectacles. Perhaps one of the most important legacies from the Middle Ages was the Magna Carta, which helped shape modern democracy.

Fun Fact: Banking was invented in medieval Europe.

It's safe to say the Middle Ages' "dark" reputation is somewhat unjustified. Lots of interesting and important changes happened in this period. Who knows where we'd be without them? However, if there's one thing we can be glad that hasn't survived from that time, it's barber-surgeons! A haircut, dentist appointment, and surgery all in one place? No thank you!

Is there anything else from the medieval era that you're glad doesn't exist today? Can you think of any areas in your life that the Middle Ages might have impacted?

Chapter 10 Activity

Time to put your new medieval knowledge to the test!

1. When did the Middle Ages take place?

2. What were the three types of medieval castles?

3. During tournaments, knights would try to knock the other rider off their horse using a lance. What was this game called?

4. What type of workers were members of guilds?

5. What was the main difference between a peasant and a serf?

6. Where did monks live?

7. What style of architecture featured vaulted ceilings, pointed arches, spires, and gargoyles?

8. What was the name of the deadly pandemic known as the Black Death?

9. Which cultural movement followed the Middle Ages?

Chapter 10 Answer

How many answers did you remember?

1. When did the Middle Ages take place? The Middle Ages took place between 500 to 1500 CE.

2. What were the three types of medieval castles? The three types of medieval castles were motte-and-bailey castles, stone keeps, and concentric castles.

3. During tournaments, knights would try to knock the other rider off their horse using a lance. What was this game called? This game was called a joust.

4. What type of workers were members of guilds? Craftsmen and merchants were members of guilds.

5. What was the main difference between a peasant and a serf? A peasant could own land or a business. A serf could not.

6. Where did monks live? Monks lived in monasteries.

7. What style of architecture featured vaulted ceilings, pointed arches, spires, and gargoyles? Gothic architecture featured vaulted ceilings, pointed arches, spires, and gargoyles.

8. What was the name of the deadly pandemic known as the Black Death? The bubonic plague was the name of the deadly pandemic known as the Black Death.

9. Which cultural movement followed the Middle Ages? The Renaissance followed the Middle Ages.

If you want to learn more about tons of other exciting historical periods, check out our other books!

VOL. 1
EUROPEAN HISTORY
FOR KIDS

A CAPTIVATING GUIDE TO THE EARLY HISTORY OF EUROPE FROM PREHISTORIC TIMES, THROUGH ANCIENT EUROPE AND THE MIDDLE AGES, TO THE RENAISSANCE AND THE AGE OF DISCOVERY

CAPTIVATING HISTORY

References

If you enjoyed this book and would like to learn more about medieval Europe, check out some of the resources below. Captivating History also has many other history books for kids. Be sure to check out our European history books that cover prehistoric times to the modern day!

Websites:

https://www.historyforkids.net/middle-ages.html

https://kids.britannica.com/kids/article/Middle-Ages/353464

https://medievaleurope.mrdonn.org/

https://www.history.com/topics/middle-ages/middle-ages

Books:

Beowulf. Available on Amazon and other major book retailers

Chaucer, Geoffrey. *The Canterbury Tales*. Available on Amazon and other major book retailers

Boyer, Crispin. National Geographic Kids Everything Castles: Capture These Facts, Photos, and Fun to Be King of the Castle! (2011).

National Geographic Kids. *National Geographic Kids Knights and Castles Sticker Book*. (2021).

Stokes, Jonathan W. *The Thrifty Guide to Medieval Times: A Handbook for Time Travelers*. (2019).

YouTube:

https://www.youtube.com/c/CaptivatingHistory

https://www.youtube.com/c/Simplehistory

https://www.youtube.com/c/EnglishHeritage